J.J. ZANA

script

translated by
Anna Magavern

bleu.

principles

I think *all*—
My body allows

What I refuse to see
Leaves me indifferent—

I may as well kill
Those who can't die

That which is lost
Transforms me—

sessions

PRE-SEQUEL

The challenge?—Add another layer of reality to the overly flat surface of events. Densify experience by covering it with a veil (sometimes imaginary) which may be its corrective, or expedient. It is not enough to walk, now—one must fly, too, and effortlessly follow the slant paths that lead to the dead *end.*

I begin to doubt as soon as I try to understand; in the exercise of my reflexivity, I take pleasure in the reflection of a thought to which I'm foreign, being at the image's origin.

All action is equal, and worthless, since it's the opposite of that emptiness we all seek in the end—or indeed finds us, flat summit at the end of the way.

I crush the memory of a fate and borrow my technique from art to sketch the state of trance into which I've sunk.

I'm pushed against an imaginary where everything accelerates and bears witness to the radiant flash of my next fall, endlessly. I repeat absence, melt into impermanence, and pretend to believe no longer in that dead god—Chance.

———

The grip of any substance on my body;
I don't try to escape;
I accept, once more, the truth of any harmony.

———

Broken line between sensation and sentiment, I traced the outline of a movement, meditated, then closed my eyes to reverse the current.

I erase a hundred centuries of hope and anticipation through the inhuman desire to let myself drop; like sunflowers in winter, I'm motionless and my heart is black.

Slowness, when it allows itself to be apprehended, becomes that positive lacuna which saturates the emotions and completes the loss of all direction.

The exhibition of a form is the most human principle, since all gods, by definition, show nothing.

Contract drafted for an alienated species, humankind signs with its neighbors a pact to represent them—by means more or less indirect. Determined to display the results of their diagrams, creators tolerate revealing themselves to face the obligations of "society."

Piano. The hand still trembles—but the mind no longer hesitates.

Surrounded by a set at once solid and fragile, a sort of support, made of paper, between the representation of reality and the evolution of being, I can only listen to the signals of the world, capture the frequencies, and lose myself in the uncorrected movement of the *strains* that run through my *veins*.

Artists offer raw material which all kinds of thinkers stumble against, reflect upon, and finally—the best ones—transmute.

A sum of experiences associated with the work of consciousness, technique is a field doomed to be forgotten at the moment of *shock*. Induced technique: veiled technique—second to song, primary.

Will breaks the tranquil course of natural effectuations, and people, stuck in it in morose astonishment, find they regret diverting the river from its original object.

Music is my matter—I sculpt time and live in squalor.

In the pure production of writing, I take stake in an adventure without knowing its structure in advance. I am with, and without, myself. Miracle of vanities, I'm in league with a figure who profanes, promises, purifies—but never lies.

The line a sky draws between two clouds: before—and after the event.

I see no other way to escape the process leading to the absolute; too many people chase in vain a purpose that will leave them *duped*.

If the poet is spellbound, it's by the mirage of being unable to resign. Forced aboard, like it or not, the ship of the one-way sign.

I sometimes feel myself drifting toward the non-irremediable loss (because sleep comes to save me) of my fundamental being so quickly, and so easily, that I start to wonder whether what I call myself might be, first and foremost, the product of my dreams.

I never achieved anything long premeditated, except the successes that broke down the essence of my uniqueness. When I have advanced in the open circle of my mortal substance, it's always been by accident.

Temporality is a *double* element that accumulates on the nature of things—like a layer of snow on a concrete road. The road was not built for winter, but the material bears the water.

I accept and even desire the circular current that makes me contemporary with what I was in my mother's womb. No will, no hesitation: I oppose the total mastery of my being (let go) to the thrall of methodic doubt, however banal, which has reigned over my mystical reason.

———

*I chose
the dream.*

———

Consciousness is not a thing built brick by brick (this is a wall) but a living entity that feeds on inversions and willingly puts itself at risk.

If the only coherence is poetry, which is color, there are only accords, never oppositions. There is a cancellation, in its essence, of the principle of contradiction.

Sound, in that it imposes a temporality on the mind, facilitates thinking; thoughts harmonize with frequencies.—

It's not the decision that is difficult, it's living with the decision... The critical moment is at d+1—or between d and d+1, when the interval that separates two antagonistic events has yet to be defined.

---

*Essences of sounds
and senses—synthesis
of a syntax.*

Placed above themselves, but only a few centimeters away, poets, enemies of patterns, *regularly* disrupt the conditions of their existence, and therefore of their art.

There is a certain pride in being invisible—which brings the self back to its proper value, and, passing it through the sieve of inaction, saves it from a certain madness.

We must learn to work fast, because we can't work long.

relations

LANES

In our small provincial city hall, the natural pool proposal was fiercely debated... First for budgetary reasons, naturally, and then in regards to the design of the pool, which some administrators wanted to be circular, and others more straight, according to convention... We finally found common ground and decided on a grand-piano-shaped structure with, at one end, two parallel swimming lanes marked off with red and white floats. Today, following a long period of construction, the pool is finally open, much to everyone's satisfaction, and above all the children's.— But: the swimmers go outside the lanes, and randomly!

SPELL

It was a little before midnight. I was at my table, after a long day—I was making some notes on a sheet of paper. In the dark park that stretched across from my balcony, closed at night, there was no sign of life, and only the sound of water running through the copper pipes of the apartment broke the silence of the lit room. Before me, in addition to my old inkwell, the usual disorder of my desk: three notebooks stacked on top of each other, a few pencils, and, in the middle of other objects, as if lost, near an old music box, the photograph of an only child, who was asleep in the next room.

The sheet of paper began to shake. Weakly at first, then faster and faster... I opened my eyes wide, moved closer: the sheet was really shaking. Slapping down my hand as if to swat an insect, with impunity, I pinned it against the desk and stopped its movement. As the sheet remained still under my tense fingers, I withdrew my hand. I closed my eyes for a second, then looked at the words on the paper: the shape of the letters was changing. The order of words, sentences, paragraphs changed before my eyes; lines were fading.

I rose from my chair and went to my balcony; sitting on a wooden stool, my head in my hands, I smoked half a cigarette, then returned to my work table. The sheet had slipped onto the floor. I examined it: it was blank. On the other side, the words had disappeared. I tried to grab the paper, but the sheet escaped, spun in the air, and landed on the window sill. I took out another sheet, tried to write again—the symbols refused to appear. I copied the same sentence twenty times over, like a student being punished by the gods, but the paper remained invariably blank. The ink flowed, but dissolved under the effect of a spell I didn't try to understand.

I stood up again. I paced around my room, staring blankly, annoyed, then examined the two hands of the clock: their circuit—its regularity—hadn't stopped.

I pulled out a third white sheet and began to draw. Even the imprint of my drawing, the tiny furrow carved by the pencil's attack, remained invisible—I went back to the balcony. Before me, four stars, forming an imperfect square, seemed to be appraising each other; I stared at them and, as if alerted by my presence, they began to change positions. Slowly, not shooting, never losing their brightness, they moved, then fell still again. I silently lit another cigarette. At the end of the sky, between two worried clouds, the moon appeared; it seemed petrified, pink in color, and I was about to trust in it when it traced, with unprecedented speed, a line parallel to the horizon. I left the balcony.

PRESENT

My sick brother gave me a book wrapped in tissue paper for my birthday last year. This year, for the same day, I received in the mail a package from him which contained the same book, wrapped in the same paper. My lover said to me, "Your brother is sick." I replied, "My brother knows I haven't read the book."

MANI

My wife is a sculptor. Her preferred materials are clay and stone, often combined. She also writes poetry, and for many years, Mani—that's her name—maintained these two disciplines, these two characters. She oscillated continuously, not forcing herself to choose, seemingly waiting for a sign that would push her onto the path to follow. She always repeated, "I like to write and sculpt equally, but you can't have everything; art is elimination."

I found this too severe, unfairly radical, but the fact is that things weren't coming.

It was a specific piece that finally disrupted this double trajectory. One day, when she got back from her studio, Mani, who is very meticulous and goes there every day from eight to one, sat down across from me and, with a shy smile, told me that sculpture had definitively imposed itself. She liked the evanescence of language, but materials were, she said, vital to her—and she added something to support her decision: "I also feel, and I could be wrong, that my sculpture is more singular; I have the sense that I'm the only person who can create it, and this feeling gives me strength."

- -

I've never wanted to take with Mani the posture of a man who, thanks to his natural distance from her work, would be able to validate or invalidate some artistic choice. I've always had complete confidence in her. There was—there still is—a calm determination in her eyes that made her future success obvious, necessary.

― ―

Mani always gets up first, and I make sure to leave her alone. I realized, after a long period of coexistence, that she needs continuity between sleep and work in order to remain in that sleepwalking state that favors creation. I get up when she leaves our house for the studio, and start my day with a hot bath. I put on some music, close my eyes, and let myself be lulled for a moment by the sway of the water. I take my time. I then lie down again for a few minutes, on a whim, then rise a second time and dress.

When Mani returns from the studio, our meal is ready. She sits down, ravenous, and tells me about the comings and goings of her morning. She insists on explaining to me with precision the thought, at once pure and labyrinthine, underlying her work. When she asks for my opinion, I question, oppose, reflect—send her back to her initial intuition. Lunches go on and on: Mani relaxes. We drink a glass of red wine; she pours a little water in hers. When she's finished purging herself of her morning session, Mani abruptly stops speaking. I tell her about the first part of my day, comment on the piece I listened to in the bath, and detail the state of the vegetables planted in the garden. Hand in hand, we go to observe the growth of tomatoes, parsley, thyme. Afternoons are calmer. Mani listens to music. She does the dishes. We sometimes bike into town to wander around or see a movie. In winter, I make a fire in the fireplace while Mani draws. When she has a show coming up, we both prepare for it—my wife insists that I'm the only one who knows how to stage her work. We choose the pieces together. The closer the show approaches, the more she turns inward—Mani changes frequency. She is elsewhere, in the center of a place I cannot access. With a floorplan of the room constantly at our fingertips, we reflect on the layout of the pieces, how to put the space in tension. It's a kind of duet.

THREAD

From a neighbor's balcony stretches a thread, white and thin, attached to a tree in the street. When night falls and light gives way to darkness, the thread disappears. Sitting on a woven wooden chair, I stare, but no longer see it. In vain I try to sharpen my perception, strain my eyes, squint—nothing helps: the thread is lost.

TALE

A prince had, from birth, a genie at his service. The genie was a devoted and honest spirit; the prince was young and ambitious. Great things perhaps awaited him. One misty winter morning, the prince, who had gone hunting in the forest on his estate, returned panting on his galloping horse. His retinue was left behind. Immediately, the genie appeared on the front steps of the castle, approached the animal and, worried, questioned the prince.

– What happened, Master?
– A terrible thing: I met the eyes of Death in the forest.
– Please, rest assured: that is no cause for concern. Every day thousands of beings meet the eyes of Death and survive; this is what we call fear.
– I know, but this time, I thought I was living my final moments. Because when our eyes met, the face of Death changed. It looked... troubled.
– Troubled?
– Yes, troubled. I can't read this omen, but I prefer to flee as quickly as possible. Prepare my things: I'm leaving for the city without delay. I will settle there for a while, amid the tumult, and return when I feel more at ease. You will stay here to watch over the estate.
– Very well.

The prince's retinue arrived behind him, and the genie slowly left the courtyard for the prince's apartments. A few minutes later, the loaded coach drove off in the direction of the city, which it reached shortly before the end of the day, and the genie remained the sole master of the abandoned estate. He first closed most of the rooms in the castle, which would remain unused in the prince's absence, then, curiously, decided to go for a walk in the forest. He too came across Death, and addressed it directly, as an equal.

– I learned earlier today that you crossed paths with my master.
– I did.
– He told me that you seemed troubled, seeing him in the forest of his own estate.
– It's true: I was troubled, or rather surprised. Because it was tonight, and in the city, that I'd planned our final meeting.

stage

"Obviously, in your words, I'm nothing but a 'bird'—hence any attempt at expression, especially under such conditions, may seem ridiculous... Nevertheless, I'm convinced that at the cost of a certain effort, above all one of logic, the animals of my species definitely have something to teach you, a message to pass on to you.—You: humans.

"I won't deny it: we spend most of our time *above* you. To your hands that handle everything, we preferred a pair of wings that propel us into the sky; the open air is our natural environment; a high vantage point is our hallmark. We always go naked, barely heavier than the feathers that cover our frail skeletons, and we are able to fly for a long time without touching solid ground. If necessary, our claws serve as feet and we tread the earth with slow, jerky steps, swinging our necks to the rhythm of the inner music that conducts us. Our brains, infinitely less powerful than yours, nevertheless fulfill their main prerogative, namely that of ensuring our survival. Our memory, which only spans a short term, makes us beings without pasts, without history—by force of circumstance, all tradition is banished from our world, but also all plans: the future being inconceivable to us, we don't waste our energy trying to predict it.

"It is our instinct that educates us, constantly... It teaches us, for example, to understand the silent language that unites our class. In one glance—we are primarily visual—we sense the direction of our comrades' flight, and thus obtain, without the slightest effort, a perfect synchrony. I know that humans have an art—or is it perhaps a sport—they call *dance*: birds enjoy it very much. One evening, perched on the roof of the opera, through the glass of the dome, I myself was able to attend a performance;

well! what dancers manage to achieve on the ground thanks to terrific discipline, we do naturally in the sky. Also, like them, we form troupes, groups that keep each other company, depending on shared affinities and aspirations. Once assembled, we travel together, perpetual nomads, unconstrained by your superficial borders, lovers of movement, seeking the beauty of flight and the favors of climate. Our migrations are a function of currents, periods of time, and, in sum, our ability to adapt to changes in our environment, which is also yours.

"Like all animals, we are not immune to vice. Eating does not pose any particular problem for us—our meager appetite is renowned—and we drink only still water, thus avoiding any mishaps. We do not blush at our wild animality, letting our very fleeting desires express themselves openly, and it is only human madness that locks us up in cages—within which we languish, deprived of our dearest, imaginary possession: freedom. On the other hand, we're chatterboxes. When we're not flying, we're rather glum, which is understandable when you've experienced the plenitude of elevation; so, to combat this spleen, we debate for hours over our territory, and I'll admit that on occasion our squabbles are a bit loud. We chirp endlessly, we chatter over trifles, and the irony is that we never draw any conclusion from our exchanges. These long negotiations are therefore useless, and it must be concluded that we chirp for the sake of chirping, without a higher goal, conservation—sorry, *conversation*—being one of our innate traits.

"Our children—and this is perhaps what constitutes the major difference between the world of humans and that of birds—our children very quickly become independent. A few days after hatching, a baby bird is already able to stand on its own, and, albeit with some apprehension, to fly for a few minutes. After having tasted this first escape, it strives each time to fly a little longer, and finally leaves the nest less than a month after its birth, and for good. All trace of the child is lost, and its progenitors pay it no mind whatsoever... Due to this hasty weaning, we have no family structure, and it sometimes happens that a mother, after this separation, meets her own offspring without recognizing them! This situation, which may seem absurd or even cruel to you, nevertheless suits us, because it grants our order an extraordinary advantage: since we cannot tell the difference between relatives and strangers, we are forced to love *all* birds."

"Speaking as a butterfly, of course I mostly agree with the remarks of my comrade the bird, but all the same it seems to me, from a critical point of view, that he has overstated the differences, exaggerated his particular virtues, and forgotten, in a text intended for humans, the main idea—namely that *we are all similar animals.*

"To justify this proposition, I would therefore like to relate, succinctly, the existence of our species, hoping that human beings will find in this account some echo of their own dispositions.

"The central event of our life is twofold: it consists of a metamorphosis. Of course, as living beings, we suffer an infinite number of transformations—every moment I change, I am no longer the same butterfly, I pass from one state to another—but on two occasions, these transformations upset the physical and mental relationship that we have with other beings, with things, with ourselves, in short completely redefining our relationship to the world.

"At birth, once we've left the egg laid by our mothers—where we began, already, this endless series of micro-evolutions—we are larvae... Confined to the ground, our bodies hairless, we discover life with wonder, although we are too slow and clumsy to grasp it. We crawl on the earth; the plant that feeds us, whose roots we brush against, seems immense to us, and when we see imagoes fly high into the air to drink nectar, we are dazzled by their majesty. For us, lowly caterpillars, not even capable of the tiniest jump, adult butterflies, endowed with the ability to fly, are like little deities that we revere, admire, and try to imitate. But a larva never lifts off! and despite all our efforts, not to mention the laborious education that is lavished on us, only one medium allows us to achieve our first real molt: *time*.

"The second stage of our life is the loneliest—and the most delicate: it separates childhood from adulthood. To better protect ourselves from possible influences on our manner of mutating, we lock ourselves in a cocoon—preferably in autumn, when the days become shorter—which we build patiently, without any help. Alone in this sheath, we meditate, fast, and watch our body transform into a nymph. This phase of physiological and psychological transition is rather sensitive; its duration varies according to the individual, and it is not uncommon for some butterflies, irritated by isolation, losing hope about reaching maturity, to give up on emerging and remain stuck in their silk prison, stalled in that difficult age. For others, on the contrary, this evolution is almost automatic: the intestines transform at full speed, the two pairs of wings suddenly erupt—which can then break through their chrysalis and propel them into the air without wobbling, ready to venture into the world of more experienced, and calmer, butterflies.

"For the third phase of our insect existence is that of blossoming. We attain our full dimensions and, for the first time, jump becomes flight. We escape this terrible gravity; our four scaled wings display splendid colors; we can finally roam the skies. Everything brightens. Our field of vision widens, the anxiety of becoming fades—it is at once the beginning and the end of the long road you humans call fate."

"We—the fleas—are always jumping. Certainly, in the eyes of birds, butterflies, or any other flying object, our leaps may seem tiny, but they are the meaning of our existence and also our one way, impulsive and discontinuous as it is, of maneuvering on earth. These random jumps, be they voluntary or reflexive, raise us for a brief moment above the ground, and take us to another point in space where we must go."

diptych

I am a painter.

After several years during which I confronted the blank canvas and then proceeded systematically toward the destruction of my unstable production, I finally came to understand that my work consisted of drawing lines.

The material is arbitrary. The support on which I establish my plans—the empty, but not silent surface that welcomes my compositions—is canvas, paper, or screen. The marker changes. The line, more or less thick, slanted or straight, is the one invariant.

My work, abstract in essence, seeks to create relationships.

Lines obsess me.—A stroke, covering the shortest distance between two points, is an image of infinity.—

Exegetes never cease to offer their interpretations: "These straight lines," the first assert, "push the boundaries of conceptuality to confront the viewer with the non-circularity of contemporary artworks." "It is a mirror of the struggle between space and time," others declare, "the artist wants to guide our eye through the reversible, apparently asymmetrical meaning of his plastic proposals." I smile without pride. I paint every night.

Color is the evidence that betrays me and brings out the contours of my singularity. Apex of my difference, it is the promise of continuity that transcends the structure of my work and reveals its coherence.

Study is central. I know I am only a link in a chain, the origin and end of which are beyond me. But the method—or fantasy—on which I base my work, and therefore my life, belongs only to me.

In my studio, objects regularly change appearance. Some, very sure of their truth, stand on the floor, between the parquet boards, while others, less sound, are better elevated. I weave among them imaginary threads—establish correspondences. Their coordinates, by chance, form a plane on which I like to move: a story.

I hear voices. Hundreds of discourses, sometimes coherent, amass in my mind and present me with all kinds of choices. The volume varies, the speed too. When one speech ends, another begins, announcing itself and attempting to create a fruitful dialectic. Rarely, silence.

—But even this silence is imaginary. When the voices hush, I still hear noise. My heartbeat. My nervous system. Car engines speeding along the cobblestones of my street. Sound is everywhere.

There is no rest. Sleep, because of dreams, solves nothing.

Some voices are authoritative, thinking themselves superior; or idealistic, claiming to lead me toward the hidden center of a multiple truth. Others place themselves in the future and settle there indefinitely: rulers of a world that never comes, their influence is immense. But the most frequent represent the past and speak in its name to defend it, or burn it down.—I listen, an unfortunate witness to the infighting of my interiority.

This polyphony causes me problems of a physical nature. My body, as it can no longer bear these sounds, reacts violently, and I sometimes vomit after too hearty a meal; the foods, additional information for my harassed organism, eliminate one another.

I've never consulted a physician—my condition suits me.

As the voices never stop their latent exchange, this dialogue with myself is perpetual, overabundant, and it is difficult for me to be perfectly focused, completely present. I have my fixations: a voice repeats the same words to me for several hours, or several days.

Phonemes bounce off the surface of my mental roads and create a spiraling echo. Future and past, in total, now form a single field.

Music is the signal that heals me—and I spend most of my days in a white-walled room, playing with the filters of a superpowered system. Herbs, which I consume in the form of tea, help me too.

It's ironic that I live alone, in a room sublet from a senile old woman—who continues to address her late husband out loud… In a way, her logorrhea offsets my silence, and her madwoman's words are the beginnings of answers to my silent monologues.

Each of my voices seems to have a dedicated place, a location of its own inside my mind. If the voice is multiform by nature, it appears fixed and enclosed from a spatial point of view. I sometimes try to draw, on a notebook with lined pages, the paradoxical diagram of my interiority; I never succeed. Matrices, labyrinths, rhizomes—the figures follow and destroy each other.

As I know several languages, exchanges become more complex and interference occurs. Modes and structures change. Vocabularies rearrange. Each voice has a preferred language; some—the most insistent—are able to switch from one to another without losing the essence of their message.

I try to decipher the signs. Words, as they are mentally uttered, are only a pretext; the voices, because they take root in a gray area of my consciousness, express themselves in images. I scrutinize their syntax, stumble on an inexplanation—and sink into the absence of action. My relationship to reality distends. The outside world is now only one possible dimension, among others. The voices become more solid. I end up attaching a face, a body to them, and move from one to the other in a cleavage that pains me.

My life is a test, since those who watch judge me. A look, even the slightest glance, is never neutral: it is an active process that engages an opinion, sometimes unconscious. It is this layer of reality that increases my anxiety, or rather precedes it—and presides over it.

My position is this: I have to constantly *prove*. To prove something—anything—to this otherness that pursues me. But I hate to convince, even myself.

after poetry

The sun reflects off the skin of my face, but light now illuminates only half of my private theater. Four days before a long-awaited death, my lost body can no longer hide behind a mediate posture, whose anchor would be the impossibility of laying down the obverse of reality. Forced to conform to the mirrors of a beauty with no school, to cross my two eyes stretched by sleepless hours and alcohol, I am obliged to concede to speech… Sketches, idols, the old doors of museums are dead, or closed.

The first look is for the one who has to leave, in spite of herself, the hopscotch game begun the day before; the second, which dives into the perfect body of a being without lucidity, is curved. Head high, but neck bent, like a swan washing its wet, white skin, shoulders slightly raised, the eyes stare at an ancient corridor and wait for the mystical race to begin. Midnight. The child prepares to condemn their hopes in order to enter the horizontal delirium coveted for nine years. To this idea, the eyes respond with a sensation that is contrary, but not opposed: knowledge, brief and cold.

Timeless borders that limit the immediate power of the present, of the real, regions of a deliberate future, I have drawn you... Nocturnal geographies, calls to travel, I rose with a lucid leap to find you, in images, near the one-way mirror of an ancient ballroom. A single speck of reality is enough, today, to make a mark—a fold—and now I can flee, in spite of myself, the distinction between fact, faith, and void... What I offer in sacrifice, besides laughter, is the reason of a man hung from a straight line—the pallid victory of desire.

pieces

One must make

One must ache

MATTER

Repetition is voluntary.

Transports aid transfers.

Invisibility is the inverse of visibility.

The elimination of time is the preliminary step to all creation.
Space comes only later.

There is a limit to speech.
It's the word: word.

FOOTAGE

What I want to touch is not visible—it has nothing in common with the truths established by my hand's five fingers. I should always aim elsewhere: miss the mark. Move in a time without function—comb through the space that would be a virgin, dimensionless psychic zone.

*

Sleep. In the middle of the snowflakes that swirl in my contemplative skies, drifting by the pines, I apprehend the aesthetic whole. On my pink table, dead flowers lie in a vase beside which, static, rest a woolen notebook and a bottle of ink.

*

Tomorrow and yesterday clash, circle, spread, and fertilize each other… The present complements itself—I dream of parallel worlds and universes based in anger.

CODE

DECONSTRUCTION
OF THE POEM
RECONSTRUCTION
OF THE POEM

CHAINS

In worried indifference, I witness the expiration of a radiant, mute era, ever more hollowed by reason which, in defiance of obsolete sources, rants, dances, and thrashes its resonant body.

*

To suffer and to smile:
two points in my drawing.

*

Preeminence of pain and delicacy: riches. Dexterity full of sweetness, wisdom; abject object, subjective and alive, marked by a past and a present.

*

Prisons of self, prisons of sound
—prisons everywhere.

*

Loss of mass and face of ice—rising dialectic of non-violence—truth is born from the unintended assent of the double that hides within all humanity.

THOUGHT

I

First apprehension of light by means of the black line, thought is the form—the force—that reduces the series of variations promoted by *seeing*.

II

Thought, which is an impersonal exercise, helps artists free themselves from a powerful empire: the self. And since thought seems intimately linked to writing (in that it is, to a certain extent, linked to language, and writing, along with silence, is the result—or catalyst—of all language), every creator is led to develop, even if vaguely, a literary practice.

III

Free of any structure, thought precedes and directs discourse. But the converse also proves true because statements, once formulated, correct the substance of thought. Constant back-and-forth, often imprecise, even fruitless, between *impression* and *expression*.—

Thought exposes, or exposes itself, and demonstrates nothing. It is the distance that separates—and connects.

MEDITATION

Signs—music. Repetitions.
Heartbeat—curves,
—functions.

LIMIT

You want to end, always, you want to close. The open, because it leaves you in suspense, transcends the limits of the scenery drawn by others. You want to end, always—you want to close.

MOVEMENT

I replace power with
absence, order with chaos, words
with the science of silence.

*

Cautious as a mother
Pushing her child
I protect my work
And fall forward.

*

Law of return
To one, to self;
At evil's origin
Any bad choice.

substances
(2021)

H

"I like the rule that corrects emotions."
Georges Braque, Notebooks

The first dose was taken on Friday, January 8, around 10 p.m.... With four or five friends, in an apartment with two bedrooms, a long kitchen where half the space was occupied by an iron shelving unit, and a bathroom I did not enter all night. On the floor, a varnished parquet of light wood; in the rooms, several hundred vinyl records—but only one sound system, unplugged. Preparation of dinner: in the back of the kitchen, cheerful music issues from a wireless speaker. As usual, I am offered to consume hashish, certainly produced in the Netherlands, mixed with tobacco; I accept. After a few inhalations, the effect is almost immediate— and takes the form of two imperatives: breathe clean air, and be alone... Despite the peremptory tone of the substance, I remain in the kitchen, but open the window. Outside: zero degrees. The apartment is located on the fourth floor of an old building, and offers a view of three interior courtyards; faced with my lack of interest in any of these surroundings, I finally excuse myself and leave the room to take my first notes.

Empty room.—Impression of accessing an elementary truth, or better, extracting it. Acceleration of heartbeats—velocity of self-reflection. The outside world continues to exist, but everything becomes cliché. Obviousness of sensations, connections, relations; doubt reduced to nonexistence, canceled by a type of truth that nothing belies.

Every human is a composer, and they are all alike. Editing noise, cut with a knife on a wooden board. Relation to the body: severity.

The others, remaining in the kitchen, seem to belong to a foreign dimension; at least five planets separate us. The rice, cooking over low heat, will be shared between all, but their intelligences seem to fight—is this their way of loving each other?—On my side, isolated, I study the geometry of reflections on the ceiling.

Writing becomes referential. (First dissociative-critical experience: I return several times to the word "referential"—add quotation marks, remove them, hesitate between -al and -el.) Alternation of multiple, sometimes contradictory states; reigning, strident, absolute multiplicity. Flux—influx—influences: gray knowledge.

. . . .

Back in the kitchen—sadness at the effect of the drug: incommunicability. Impossibility of expressing the slightest emotion. At the moment of speaking, a wall presents itself. No passage—no sharing possible. Inanity of the collective dose; drugs are in fact a fundamentally isolating experience, even when taken together. We could imagine, by analogy, a cinema where we would bring together spectators, each watching their own film, projected on the back of the seat in front of them. Indeed, this is how airplanes today are designed: individual-plural travel.

....

Rise—fall—rise: it's almost schematic. A state of jubilation, elevation, arrival (but where? and why?)—precedes a panic attack... Witnessing such chaos, such a lack of harmony between people and things becomes downright scandalous. Should I intervene? And am I even entitled to do so? No, better let the others sink into misunderstanding, and me with them... Incomprehensible restart—but which nonetheless offers me a new certainty (hash-madness is decidedly the omnipresence of self-evident facts, even when they annihilate each other): that my calm is an exterior element, perfectly artificial—my "meditation" a farce. Once again: no mediation possible.

....

The first gestural repetitions appear; twice I extend my arm for a glass of water, twice I don't reach it. Yet it is less than a meter from me. Self-reflection, this time in the midst of others. Will to recover, to put on a good face; after the obviousness, the speed of sensations.

....

They came to deliver codes to me at the door of the apartment—solutions to three-variable equations of the type $M+N=A$. But I did not have to move to receive the information, which arrived in the form of a mental package. Flashes of meaning then crossed me. Immediately after: oblivion. Erasure, pure and simple, of the resolution. New problem: immediate solution. Hesitations about the consistency of inner reality: inability to *fix* a vibration. Back-and-forth between high and low, known and unknown: constant change. Joy, perhaps; celebration.

....

Disarmaments. Reality slips—absurdity, nonsense has taken over. Beings evaporate in speech or action.

....

In the second bedroom, one man tattoos the leg of another, lying on his stomach. The irreversibility of such a gesture fascinates me; we all look at each other, silent, helpless witnesses of this transformation. Then I ask myself: am I also undergoing an irreversible metamorphosis?*

....

Sonic hallucinations. Glances at my friends to see if they, too, are enduring the growls of an animal hidden in the cramped kitchen. Another pass—paranoia: I am the only one who does not know that a raccoon or a guinea pig is being raised here, perhaps several: an entire family of mammals trapped in the darkness of the boxes on the shelf, disturbed by our small group's conversations.

With each hallucination, I turn to the owner of the apartment and silently beg him to hear these groans. Indifference. No one with me. Solitude.

....

Three or four hours later, the effect subsides. I drank a lot of water (or tea) to dilute the mixture running through my blood. When, in the second bedroom, I refuse a line of cocaine, its inhabitant (freshly tattooed) asks me: "You don't do drugs?"—

....

Definitive return to reality. Violent in general. A lot of noise all the same, for few concrete results. Silence: never.

....

On the deserted subway platform, the impression of floating. I sit down on an iron bench—and the thirteen-minute wait passes in a flash. In the train, my neighbors appear and disappear in a sort of waltz, organized by and for me. The bodies of others, less than a meter away, move through me. Sensitivity especially to odors. If the man retreats, continues on his way, all is well; if he approaches to begin an undesired exchange, I am armed and free to react.

*I was not wrong to ask myself this question, although I only understood its meaning four days later, during a strange bout of insomnia... As I dozed on my recliner while leafing through a book on sculpture, a rose quartz lamp was lit. I woke up soon after, and climbed up to bed to sink definitively into slumber. The lamp remained lit. As I could not manage to fall back asleep, I eventually opened my eyes again; the pink light of the lamp *became* the sculpture... I thus found myself bathed in the material, caught in the composition (in process) of an unknown master. Conscious that I could not sleep in such conditions, but curious about this prison of invisible and artistic bars, I lived a real torture until my descent from the mezzanine (after much prevarication) to turn off the light. Back in my bed, the darkness soothed me—but a new truth emerged: I had become the sculpture. The master was shaping me; I felt their work on my face, specifically the region at the top of the nose, near the eyebrows. The chisel carved my skin, leaving indelible traces that I would find the next day in the mirror; it was now impossible for me to escape my condition of *artwork*... Eager to regain my calm and, truth be told, a bit afraid, I finally turned on a light (a different lamp, to avoid any relapse) and gave up on sleep for a large part of the night.

When one is not, like me, a "regular" hemp consumer, each dose is an event, a ritual, an ordeal... Since addiction to cannabis is weak,* the body easily forgets the sensations provoked by the substance and is captured, almost every time, by its unpredictable effects... The path to consumption always begins with a road: the one I need to take, real or virtual, to secure my supplies... I buy my drugs in micro-quantities, and almost always in the same place. The experience begins while I walk toward this concrete destination: in the street, surrounded by strangers who do not know what I'm preparing for, I envision the delicious moment when I'll light my first cigarette. As in art, the process that leads to delirium is as important, if not more, than the delirium itself: establishing the conditions to take narcotics defies the very notion of a narcotic by integrating it into a chosen reality, function of a subjective law. In the philosophy of yoga, it is said that herbs can permit the attainment of perfection, liberation, or the erasure of impermanence, whatever you call it; meditation is another means. But these techniques, which are two ways of accessing the same truth, are not exclusive. The second dose takes place in my studio—facing the blank page—and with music.

Whereas in a group I am seized by an irreducible desire to open myself to others, when I am alone I find this social inclination unimaginable... With the kilometers of interior life that *h* makes it possible to explore, it seems absurd to me to turn toward any external element that would not be quiet. The other, if they were able to hush, could share in the essence of my drift—but friendship, in its power, renders the state of silence practically inaccessible.

It seems that excitement, which I believed particular to the drug, is rather caused by otherness. Even at the physical level, I do not feel the speed that surrounded me during my first dose. I am coated in an extreme slowness, which characterizes even rapid gestures, and this perhaps because I break them down into a series of primary moments, all immediate—and the immediate has no speed.

I know what I want to taste, where I want to go. In fact, I don't need a large dosage, but I often add, in my mix of grass and tobacco, tea leaves, or dried flowers (lotus, damiana, rose petals, etc.)

Also: would I like to get moving for an hour, or for a day? Have I informed my circle that I will be absent?—But do I even have a circle? In hemp, more than elsewhere, absence...

The principal motive of action is now harmony. The search for harmony. In the studio that I occupy for a limited time, I move plants, objects—reshufflings that continue until I reach the desired vibration.

Once again, it's fairly schematic: action—non-action. Against the ternary movement of the first phase is opposed, when smoking alone, a duality—which will certainly have to be overcome later… For the moment, I rest in this double reality and ask myself before each gesture: should I act? Should I answer in the affirmative to the impulse which, rushing my body from its rest, wanted to push me towards movement?—The mind-body distinction, despite this alternation, or ambivalence, makes no sense; I feel no solidarity with this mixture of blood and skin with which I usually identify.

The one mirror in the space, when I come across it, reveals infra-sensitive things to me: muscle tension, brightness of organs, courses of thought.

I do not consider the writing I submit to as an "action"… As it was planned upstream of experience, it is an automated modality of my consciousness, which in some way finds its extension in the signs that I erase.

The more I express myself, the more I manage to express myself, the more it becomes clear that the multiplicity of words is language's way of struggling within a monochrome reality. Hence the fact that all writing is a cry. And how could it not be: there is nothing to say.—

The obviousness of silence (of music) almost hurts.

Adjustment of the utility principle; that's what I was referring to when I tried to describe the imperative of action. Fundamental concern: does the gain generated by the movement that I am going to initiate justify the energy I will have to mobilize? It is this economic perception (gain/loss) of reality that must be transcended.

....

This is the middle of the experience; I'm at the heart of the thing. The substance has now taken up residence in my body—it is the one that directs me. I am the puppet of a medicinal herb, which provides me a more or less brutal experience. The search for external harmony is only a metaphor for the invisible symphony, silent and sly, that is playing in my body.

....

A step back.—Why did I write (and leave) the word "sly"? Yet I don't perceive any dissimulation. Flowers never lie; they are and remain the reflection of the land where they grew and the care they received. Marijuana promises nothing—it exists, that's all—and for that reason, it is beyond reproach.

Taking sense.—Each element gradually finds its natural place in the order that directs movement. There is no longer even a question of the mystical, or the physical; reality, in its unity, becomes a truth *that must not be denied*... This is the imperative of enlightenment. The totalitarianism of lightning. The authoritarian aspect of the drug becomes concrete on the most basic subjects; initially, it leaves room for reason, which glady unfolds—only to be thrown against the ropes. Reason staggers, then collapses.

Critical work redoubles, despite the avowed absence of aesthetic ambition.

I *want* to see the contradictions—but it is the word totality that appears. Criticism splits the self, whose mistrust for unity is innate: as a child, I was not another.

....

After two hours of drifting, the first real contemplation... At the sound of Indian music, composed by Alice Coltrane, the impression of being superimposed on the recording studio—and the desire to stay there.

....

I am exhausted. The third dose of hemp overwhelmed me. I was projected into a second universe, made only of sound. I am again taken within an invisible sculpture, etc.

In my hot water, to try to recover, I squeezed half a lemon.

Physical reality of writing.—The body carries out the work which thought conceives. Fatigue is now redoubled, for euphoria has passed.

*This is the thesis of certain physicians, and of Henri Michaux...—but is it really so? It certainly seems that cannabis addiction falls more within the psychological realm than the physical—but is the former less real, or dreadful? In Michaux's work, while mescaline and LSD are, clearly, scientific experiments, limited in time or space, hemp seems rather to be a matter of custom, or practice; the conditions of the doses seem less precise than in the case of other drugs—which is in agreement with the diffuse action of h: an effect that is opaque, although systematic, and intrinsically open... An effect whose benefits or harms may be felt later—for example the next day, as was the case for me this time. The day after the experiment, although I had prepared my resin at noon, I ultimately decided to enjoy my day on an empty stomach; at one o'clock, in the middle of the street, I burst into tears... I had learned, by chance, of the death of a neighbor whom I had known, or rather, had often crossed paths with, and who had been sick for many years... A sort of altar had been erected for him by the door of a building—I stopped there, shocked, then isolated myself from curious passers-by. The crying stopped after three or four minutes, but resumed later. I don't know how I would have taken the news in a "normal" state—but I believe I had not cried such tears for a long time. There is a hypersensitivity (especially emotional) linked to hash; a play on memory, too—that same evening, I could not recall the event.

I've opened the gates of hell. This is the third session in three days—and the last; waiting for the next delirium is far too hard. I was naïve to believe in the relative harmlessness of h; *in my room, it has monopolized everything... Each object is infused with my excesses, and seems to have become fixed in place. Everything brings me back to the drug. I can no longer leave my house. No matter how much my friends insist, I put off any meeting until tomorrow to plunge into the delights of my alienation. The part of the worst that governs the soul cannot destroy it—I marvel at an evil from which I thought I no longer suffered.*

Each plant is unique. Hence, no two doses are ever identical. What I was yesterday, I already am no longer—but drawing has done me good. I drew *active* lines on about sixty pages of my notebook, or even eighty. I would be lying if I said I didn't care about the result—but once again, I felt no doubt. The stroke had the look (the speed) of the obvious; in drawing, as in writing, an automated, rather than automatic process. It's always the same: we believe a process to be immediate, when it is the sum or the product of all past experiences. The present, beyond any determinant, is only a permanent result—which in turn becomes a datum for the next product.

Drugs frighten. Human beings do not want to see totality, that is, solitude; they prefer commerce. To begin, therefore, I needed to reassure myself: "It will all be fine," I thought, "you will write in the past tense, and time, which disappeared yesterday, will protect your delirium." I convinced myself of what I already knew—I can smoke my gram without shaking. Tomorrow, I will see; I will go to the lake, or the forest, or any other natural activity; for the moment, I still want timelessness.

Artists are above all dependent on their art; it is action that best relieves their natural tension… Drugs, for them, are only the substitute for a greater addiction, which is the effort to write, or to play… As they cannot constantly be in a state of creation (that pious dream: to make one's life a work of art), they compensate with substances for a reality based on absence. They discover a certain practice—they rush into it—then suffer… Because creation follows a cyclical logic, and, incapable of rest, those who undertake it intoxicate themselves to forget (or better understand) the gap that separates artifice from art.*

*I wrote these three fragments *before* beginning the experiment—which I finally gave up. I no longer really saw the point of provoking a nightmare, since I was visibly in that state of mind... Writing, too, had calmed me down; the projection of delirium, via the literary process, had appeased my need for delirium. What I did not mention is that the day after the second experiment, a friend came to my house to consume hash. We smoked, aimlessly and without interruption, *for six hours*—and I was most often the driving force... I was the victim of disturbing visions, persistent fantasies, and ridiculous regressions; hence the third session.

APPENDIX

Some time has passed and one thing is clear: my relationship with drugs has changed. The dark-sacred side that I saw and lived during these three experiments, I can no longer forget—and I can now differentiate between recreational use and in some sense creative, or curative use.

It is only through a retroactive effect of thought that one can discriminate between intention and non-intention: believe in the influence of intentionality on the substance of reality. Indeed, one must have experienced (or, and this is more twisted, imagined) said reality to be able to judge it.

The object of these sessions was not "me"—but the drug. While habitually, people allow themselves to be visited by substances (passive principle), in the case of these experiments, from the moment I wrote the first words, it was I who went to meet hashish (active principle). It was I who moved to be on *its* terrain, in order to leave it, by making my body a conductor (of its current, of its heat), total freedom of action.

The drug was the variable—I was a constant (or the expression) of the function. Strange rigor, severe letting go which perhaps is not compatible with the activity of writing, but which I imposed on myself in order to *take stock*—and without a doubt, I needed it.

CBD

"It is the same with peyote as it is with everything human. It is a magnetic and marvelous principle, provided one knows how to take it, that is to say, in the desired doses and according to the desired gradation. And above all, not at the wrong time and out of place."

Antonin Artaud, The Tarahumaras

Following these first experiments, I decided, for several weeks, to replace my hash with CBD—a substance whose THC level is, by regulation, less than 0.3%... Of less psychoactive influence, and naturally less addictive, the extract nevertheless provoked in me the appearance of a form, *whose mischievous character possessed me for a time—then escaped.*

I pronounce
Phrases

I produce
Traces

*

What rhythms?
—Ternary

I am in
Misery

*

Twenty-one
Past six

I roam the
Abyss

A tranquil
Morning

In my bed
Mourning

*

The music
Is found

And silence
Is sound

*

The noise is
Violet

Blood of a
Violin

APPENDIX

While, out of caution, I had always kept away from synthetic drugs, these initiations, once again, transformed my conscious relationship to substances to such an extent that I experimented—alongside my consumption of CBD, and still applying that "art of doses" on which Deleuze and Guattari also insist—with ketamine, methadone, and speed... There is no need to dwell on these experiences, but I had definitely opened a portal that seemed to offer me a new tolerance,* and would lead me to the end of my experimentation...

*It is not so much a matter of physical tolerance to substances as of psychological tolerance *to the idea of substances*—that is to say, to the fact of accepting in advance that a dose is even possible... When I was younger, my categorical refusal to dip into so-called "hard" drugs seemed to stem from obedience to an external precept (medical/societal), which prohibited me from considering the possibility of any consumption. But there is another hypothesis, equally valid: I was *afraid*.—

DMT

"If, in an experiment, one does not risk their reason, the experiment is not worth trying."

Paul Éluard, Let See

The party had started, I believe, in the middle of the afternoon—but I arrived a few hours later, at the same time as a young painter who spent the whole night hunched over a sheet of paper.

The next day, around three or four o'clock, my host began to smoke an extract of dimethyltryptamine. It was Sunday. We were stretched out on old, long sofas, arranged on a rooftop terrace—the sun was coldly shining. A first time, then a second, I refused to draw on the pipe which contained the substance, while the man, inhaling several puffs on his own, assured me of its perfect quality…

Unnecessary assurances, for his face, open, relaxed, confirmed to me the veracity of the fact—

His friend, who had consistently refused to smoke throughout the eighteen-hour party, asked to have some; the man went to fetch, enclosed in kraft paper, a kind of white, luminous powder, which he placed at the end of the pipe. I asked to smell the drug; I liked the odor. The woman took a first puff, not without difficulty, then a second, longer one, which the man seemed to approve of… He was now sitting cross-legged on the floor of the terrace, in the middle of our little group: he was looking at me.

The sky was blue, cloudless—before leaving, the painter had placed his drawing, upside down, on a speaker in the living room… When, for the third time, after having emptied then replaced the powder, my host suggested that I consume dmt, my reflex was to refuse—but I spoke the words with so little will, or determination, that the man, delighted with the doubt I had unveiled, moved closer with the bong.*

It was he who took my hand to close the opening of the glass piece, and thus allow a sufficient amount of smoke to collect. Then, for a final approval, he met my eyes, which I closed in a sign of consent.

My initiator burned the powder with a gas lighter, and I deliberately drew in half a dose. Maybe more. The substance went straight to my thymus. The man then pulled on the pipe and spat out the smoke with a smile—I finally exhaled.

....

One can distinguish two types of frequencies, which are also interrelated: a first, internal, which concerns the body, and a second, external, which relates to the space, or field, which surrounds the body—drugs exert an influence on both frequencies. The object, in any case, and for everyone, is to find the frequency which allows, while maintaining a position of equilibrium, the highest degree of freedom—and, more difficult still, to extend it, or apply it, that is to say, to tune the world to this vibration.

But as it is vain, and moreover violent, to believe that a body can constantly impose its power on other bodies, the question is also how to make the different frequencies coexist. And whether the external frequency (that of space) can accept multiplicity. Because if it is possible that the field, at any given time, only delivers a single vibration, one can also posit the principle of a plural vibration that space always works to create.—

*It is impossible for me to say whether I created this opening involuntarily. For while it is true I had never imagined I would take dmt that day (it was the first time, and I did not know that my host had some), it is obvious that the conditions were *ideal*... It is difficult to contest what is there, to deny the brutality of reality, such that I could not ignore, despite all the timeless calculations, the secret rituals, the shared experiences of death or rebirth—I could not ignore that the naked truth of dmt was in front of me, and I only had to reach out my hand to collect it.

Appendix

After this unexpected afternoon, I was disoriented for three or four days... I wandered my neighborhood aimlessly, marked by the intact sensation of the substance infusing my heart. It seemed to me that this act, like this tattoo or that wound, had branded me, and that the burn, superficial yet exact, would leave an indelible mark... But isn't this ultimately the case *for any contact*? Anyway, it was not until much later, finally in tune with the substance, that I began to meditate on the sense of these three words:

duration—mass—tao.

akai

From the slightest tension
Of a soul
The poem is born

*

On the blue ground
Of spring
A shadow passes

*

Stand up straight
Against the gods—
And wait

*

I see myself alive
And dead—
Deep sleep

*

There is nothing
More
Than chance

states

BALL

Yesterday, early in the night, I made a pact with fire, or the devil—and I can consequently affirm that things will behave a bit better from now on... The dread of losing the beloved object; the fear, the awful fear of shining; all the desire lost in the infinity that separates humanity has submerged—the candle burned—and reality, in some way, turned.

CORRESPONDENCE

Color, in actuality, is not applied to the surface. Color is contained in the space that separates surfaces,—it is the continuous vibration that permits contrasts.

        She would like
        To grow

It is perfectly possible that the law of attraction which conditions the coming together of beings and objects is a weak law, in terms of magnitude, and that the fields of "finitude" consist of imaginary, albeit reliable, vibrations, conceived and painted on a green screen…

        I don't want
        To know

Which is?—Two children, white and gray, audacious, stationed in the first row of the banquet,—plus a naked feast savored upside down, in slow motion, walking on the hands of thought.

DIRTY

It is night—time is in tune. I cling to a flat and dirty style before the oblivion of all friendship. Unanswered questions, pointless motions—I continue, badly and well, to make drawings. Dancer and water, water and dancer: I try to find, on paper, the whiteness of an elsewhere. I marvel; I work small, short, textual. I make *actual* the promises of tomorrow—clutch the wind as it evaporates between my hands,—and set the scene for an experimental project. But: I commit the primal error of not showing the self, even—of being outside a system. Then comes an irrepressible need to apologize; doubt; fear—and finally fear of fear.

TURIYA

THERE IS A FOURTH STATE BEYOND THE TRIPLE AND VISIBLE DIMENSION OF REALITY—I AM THAT STATE IF I AM THE WAY OF IMMATERIALITY. IN A WORLD WITHOUT GOD, I NOW MOVE IN THE HOLLOW OF AN EMPTY EXPERIENCE AND SUBMIT TO THE LAWS OF A SILENT DECADENCE. PHYSICS OF THOUGHT—OLD MODELS—COMBATS— I CURL BENEATH THE SHEETS AND WATCH THE DAY WHILE OTHERS, LESS EARLY TO RISE, KNEAD THE DOUGH WHICH THE OVEN WILL GROW. THIRTEEN HOURS HAVE PASSED SINCE THE FRIEND'S DEPARTURE—I LISTEN TO THE VARIATIONS OF A ZITHER AND INVOKE PARADISE. I BELIEVE—I CREATE—I BELIEVE I CREATE STRUCTURES BUT IN FACT UNDO THEM—OVERRIDE THE EVIDENCE OF SENSATIONS TO LET MYSELF BE CARRIED BY SOUND. I DENY ANY CONTRADICTION. I LACK THE STRENGTH TO PRONOUNCE FORM AND FUNCTION—CAN NO LONGER HIDE BEHIND THE MASK OF REPETITION. I PLAY—I PLEASE. I PUSH TWO FINGERS INTO MY ANUS—I WANT MORE. STUBBORN AND POISED, I KISS DEMON EYES AND DEMONSTRATE NORMAL INANITY—STARE AT DEAD FETUSES TO EXTRACT VIOLENT OR BANAL IMAGES. MAJOR ARCANA—DANGEROUS GAME. FIRE IN AIR—WATER IN FIRE. ELEMENTAL ARTISTRY AND LACK OF GRAVITY—THE FOURTH STATE IS A PLACE.

TITLE

It is the subconscious which, saturated, irritated by the omnipotence of the self, destroys statements, plans and laws.—

FIDEM

A fidelity that is imposed on me is an enslavement: I can only be loyal to that which I have *chosen*—hence there is no such thing as fidelity to family, for example... Moreover, fidelity is a reciprocal principle: a human alone in the world could develop the concept of rule, custom or habit—not that of fidelity. The latter is therefore based on a living object—no more is it possible to have true fidelity to a value, or to a god... It is possible, conversely, to show fidelity to a friend, a lover, an animal, or a plant—and then we have, as the word suggests, faith in them.—But what do we have faith in when we are loyal to that being, chosen among all? In fact, we *put* faith in them—to have chosen us too. What I respect today, in the practice of my fidelity, is primarily the choices made by an other for the me of yesterday—whose limits I know so well. Fidelity is anachronistic: it makes a past agreement triumph over a present event called betrayal, or the will to betray.

URGENCY

It appears that the boundary between poetry and madness is constituted by a certain kind of resilience. A dangerous line in itself, since resilience is no stranger to pride, which tends toward delirium.

The gaze of others terrifies precisely those for whom it serves as a driving force.—We aren't alone because we work: we work because we are essentially alone.

Double combat of art: acquisition of a technique, and search for the self, through the self. The process of individuation comes to redoubles the practice of art—and, paradoxically, gives it its universal character.

The creative process is a progressive, internal divorce of the powers that govern the artist's body.

Like physics, art seems to follow two distinct sets of laws: a first, intellectual, prosaic, based on gravity—and a second, instinctual, poetic, whose point of departure and of arrival is mystery.

The free pursuit of instincts is a liberation—which enslaves. But those who know no master, and distrust even themselves, know that everything, even slowly, moves *before* them... It is the one-sidedness of fate that must be grasped: this straight and dry force that action puts in motion, then cancels.

script

The scene before the credits is in black and white. The credits and quote are in white characters, on a black background. The rest of the film is in color.—

EXT. RIVER - DAY

Music.

A teenager emerges half-naked from a river that could be the Thames. Gray sky, white light. On the grassy bank reclines a thirty-year-old man, reading a newspaper... He is dressed respectably, in thick black trousers that show his ankles and a white shirt, open at the collar. His shoes and hat are placed beside him. It is the poet Paul Verlaine. The teenager approaches him, bends over, and shakes his wet hair to splash him.

Laughter.

The teenager lies down, too, and positions himself so as to rest his head on his lover's belly: the two bodies are perpendicular.

After a brief moment of gazing at the sky, as if bored, he stretches out his arm to search for matches in the heap of his clothes, strikes one with a smile—then sets fire to Verlaine's paper, making him leap up and scream.

- -

"Hadn't I once *a youth that was lovely, heroic, fabulous, fit to be written on pages of gold?—Too much luck! Through what crime, by what fault did I deserve my present weakness? You who claim that animals sob with sorrow, that the sick despair, that the dead dream badly, try now to relate my fall and my sleep.*"

Arthur Rimbaud, A Season in Hell

SCRIPT

PRINCIPLES	7
SESSIONS	13
RELATIONS	23
STAGE	35
DIPTYCH	45
AFTER POETRY	53
PIECES	59
SUBSTANCES	73
AKAI	115
STATES	119
SCRIPT	129